D1390320

A HORRID FACTBOOK

HORRID HENRY'S SPORTS

Francesca Simon

Illustrated by Tony Ross

Orion
Children's Books

First published in Great Britain in 2012
by Orion Children's Books
This new edition published in Great Britain in 2014
by Orion Children's Books
a division of the Orion Publishing Group Ltd
Orion House
5 Upper St Martin's Lane
London WC2H 9EA
An Hachette UK company

1 3 5 7 9 10 8 6 4 2

Text © Francesca Simon 2012, 2014
Illustrations © Tony Ross 2012, 2014

The moral right of Francesca Simon and Tony Ross to be
identified as author and illustrator of this work has been asserted.

Facts compiled by Sally Byford.

All rights reserved. No part of this publication may be
reproduced, stored in a retrieval system, or transmitted,
in any form or by any means, electronic, mechanical,
photocopying, recording or otherwise, without the
prior permission of Orion Children's Books.

The Orion Publishing Group's policy is to use papers
that are natural, renewable and recyclable products
and made from wood grown in sustainable forests.
The logging and manufacturing processes are expected
to conform to the environmental regulations
of the country of origin.

ISBN 978 1 4440 1288 0

A catalogue record for this book
is available from the British Library.

Printed in Great Britain by
Clays Ltd, St Ives plc

www.orionbooks.co.uk
www.horridhenry.co.uk

CONTENTS

Hello from Henry

Hey gang! Welcome to my absolutely fantastic new book about all things sporty. And when I say all, I mean — all! Like info about the World Cow Poo throwing contest, and what kind of smelly competitions they used to have in ancient Japan, and not forgetting the slimiest sport ever, the Bog Snorkling Championships.

Yup, it's all here, and more. I've gathered together the most fascinating and surprising sports facts ever. Because, let's face it, who wouldn't rather stretch out on a sofa crunching crisps and guzzling fizzywizz drinks while reading about *other* people running and jumping and wrestling like lunatics?

Have fun!

Henry

PS — you might not recognise weird measurements like 'yards' from the old imperial system, but they're used for traditional sports like rowing.

FIRST FACTS

The word **'sport'** comes from an old French word – 'desport' – meaning 'leisure'.

Paintings of wrestlers have been discovered on the walls of an **Egyptian tomb** from around 1850 BC – which means wrestling was probably one of the **earliest sports** ever played.

There are now about **8,000** known sports and sporting games around the world.

Today, the top five **most popular sports** watched worldwide are football, cricket, field hockey, tennis and volleyball.

But more people take part in **fishing** worldwide than in any other sport.

Popular American sports like baseball, basketball and American football don't make it into the top five – they are big in the USA, but less popular in other parts of the world.

The Summer Olympics is the **most famous sporting competition** in the world – it happens once every four years.

4.7 billion TV viewers watched the Beijing 2008 Olympic Games and Paralympic Games. That's nearly three out of every four people in the entire world!

Taking part in sport makes people healthier and happier.

ACTION-PACKED PAST

Football was invented in China around 476 BC.

The 'ancient' Olympic Games were first held in 776 BC, as a religious festival to honour Zeus, king of the Greek gods.

For many years, there was **just one race** at the Olympics – a running race of 192 metres. It was from one end of the stadium to the other, about the same length as today's **200 metre** sprint race.

In 490 BC, a Greek soldier delivered a message to Athens from **a place called Marathon**. He ran 171 miles in just two days – and the Marathon race was invented and named after his achievement.

Romans enjoyed **watching people die** – for entertainment! They went to amphitheatres to see **gladiators** fight to the death.

Too bad Miss Battle-Axe wasn't around then. Or Soggy Sid.

Roman wrestling was rough! **Biting**, **kicking** and **scratching** were all allowed – you were only disqualified if you poked someone's eye out.

The ancient Olympic Games were banned by the **Romans** in 393 AD because they refused to worship the Greek gods.

The modern-day Olympic Summer Games were started again in 1896 by Frenchman Baron Pierre de Coubertin, who wanted to encourage young people to take part in sport.

William the Conqueror's favourite sport was **hunting** – but anyone who dared to kill the king's deer lost his life or his eyesight.

James II banned golf in Scotland because he was preparing for an English invasion and he wanted everyone to practise archery instead of **wasting their time** playing golf.

Hockey was a popular European sport in medieval times, and its name comes from the **French word** 'hocquet', meaning 'shepherd's crook' because this is what a hockey stick looks like.

Surfing started over **three thousand years ago** when fishermen in Western Polynesia discovered that **riding waves** on a wooden board was a great way of getting their fish to shore.

Queen Elizabeth I thought football was a very rough sport – she disliked it so much that if she caught anyone playing the game, she **threw them into jail**.

The first Oxford-Cambridge Boat Race took place in 1829. Two friends had the idea – Charles Merivale, a student at Cambridge, and Charles Wordsworth, who was at Oxford.

Table tennis started as after-dinner entertainment in Victorian England. Posh people called it **'wiff-waff'** or **'ping-pong'** because of the sound the balls made on the racquets.

Until the Eighteenth Century, fox hunters in England galloped across open fields. But when fences were built to divide up the land, both the horses and the riders had to learn to jump – and **show jumping was born**.

Until the Nineteenth Century, football was played **in the streets**. For some football matches, the captains' houses – often several streets apart – were used as goals.

FASCINATING FIRSTS

England players first wore their **names on the back of their shirts** during the 1992 European Championships in Sweden.

The first Wimbledon Tennis Championship took place in 1877 when it was watched by 200 spectators. Now it's broadcast to over **one billion people** every year.

Martina Navratilova was the **first player** to win the women's singles tennis title at Wimbledon **nine times**.

In 1976, Nadia Comăneci of Romania was the first gymnast to score a **perfect ten** in an Olympic competition – in fact, she scored a grand total of **seven perfect tens!**

Kung fu was first practised in **China** in 527 AD by **monks** – now people do it all over the world.

The first Olympic 100 metres champion was an American, Thomas Burke, who won the 1896 race in Athens in 12 seconds. The current record is much faster – 9.58 seconds, held by Usain Bolt.

In 1804, Alicia Meynell was the first woman to compete in a two-horse horse race in England. She rode **four miles** side-saddle, but was pipped to the post by her opponent.

The **1948 London Olympics** were the first Games people could watch at home on TV.

Yippee! My kind of fact.

In the early 1960s, the first skateboards were just **planks of wood** with rollerskates nailed to them.

The first puck ever used in a hockey game was a frozen piece of **cow dung**.

At the 1985 German Grand Prix, the first **live on-board camera** was attached to a Formula One driver's race car. Today, all F1 cars are fitted with at least five cameras.

Hawk-Eye – a camera used to track the direction and speed of balls – was first used in 2001 by Channel 4 during a cricket match between England and Pakistan.

In 2007, Hawk-Eye was used for the first time at the Wimbledon Lawn Tennis Championships to tell if a ball was in or out.

In 1954, Roger Bannister was the first man to run a mile in **under 4 minutes**.

I bet even Aerobic Al couldn't beat that.

Trevor Francis was the first footballer to earn a **one million pound** transfer fee when he signed to Nottingham Forest in 1979.

In 2009, the highest ever transfer fee was paid when Cristiano Ronaldo signed to Real Madrid for £80 million.

You know, I'd accept half that.

WICKED
WINNERS

Only **four football teams** have ever finished at the top of the Premier League – Arsenal, Manchester United, Chelsea and Blackburn Rovers.

One day Ashton Athletic will make it five . . . with the help of Hot Foot Henry of course.

In 1960, at the Rome Olympics, Ethiopian runner Abebe Bikila won the gold medal in the Marathon – running in **bare feet!**

Ouch!

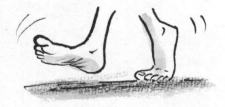

Rower, Sir Steve Redgrave, is Britain's most successful Olympic athlete of all time. He was the first athlete to win gold medals at five Olympics in a row.

For winning the women's singles at Wimbledon in 1966, Billie Jean King was given a £25 gift voucher. The winner in 2011, Petra Kvitova, received over **a million pounds!**

Just think how much chocolate that would buy.

In 1904, American gymnast, George Eyser, won **six Olympic medals**, including one for rope climbing, even though he had a **wooden leg.**

American cyclist, Lance Armstrong, recovered from a life-threatening illness to win the Tour de France **seven times in a row** between 1999 and 2005.

German race car driver, Michael Schumacher, holds the record for winning the Formula One World Championships the most times – he is a **seven-time World Champion**.

In 2003, British eventer, Pippa Funnell, won the three major horse riding competitions in a row and became the **only rider** ever to win the Grand Slam of Eventing.

At the Beijing Olympics in 2008, He Junquan, a Chinese swimmer with no arms, amazed everyone by winning two gold medals and one silver.

UK's Paula Radcliffe has won the London Marathon **three times**. She set the women's world marathon record in 1993 at 2 hours 15 minutes and 25 seconds, and **no one has broken it yet**.

I wonder if she used my sneaky sweet-dropping trick to distract her opponents.

CHAMPION CHEATS AND LOVEABLE LOSERS

Eddie 'the Eagle' Edwards, a British skier, came bottom in both of his ski jumping events at the 1988 Winter Olympics. He was wearing a **borrowed ski-suit** and his glasses were so steamed up he couldn't see where he was going!

When American Helen Stephens beat Poland's Stella Walsh to second place in the Olympic 100 metres, Stella claimed that Helen was **really a man**. Helen had to remove her clothes to prove she was a woman!

In the 1908 Olympics, Italian Dorando Pietri was declared the winner of the Marathon, even though he **collapsed five times** and had to be helped across the finish line by policemen and attendants!

In 1904, Fred Lorz won the Olympic Marathon – but his gold medal was taken away when it was revealed that he'd **ridden in a car** for 11 miles of the race!

Great idea – I must remember that for sports day.

At the 2000 Sydney Olympic Games, Eric 'the Eel' made a splash when he swam 100 metres in the slowest time ever recorded, around 1 minute 52 seconds. The gold medal winner that year swam it in just under **48 seconds**.

In 1966, a Welsh rugby match between teams from Colwyn Bay and Portmadoc had to be abandoned at the last minute – because neither team owned **a ball!**

In 1984, at the Oxford–Cambridge Boat Race, Cambridge sank before the race had even begun – they hit a barge on their way to the start.

BIG AND
BEEFY

Sumo wrestling is only practised professionally in Japan. The aim of the game is to knock your opponent to the floor or out of the ring, so the **bigger and heavier** you are, the better!

Sumo wrestlers live together in training stables, where their meals, exercise and clothes are strictly controlled. They eat lots of rice and protein food and then sleep to build up their weight.

Bet Greedy Graham would like to be one — if they ate lots of sweets too.

An average grown man weighs around 80 kilograms, but sumo wrestlers weigh up to **280 kilograms!**

I wonder if one of them would like to come over and squish Margaret.

Olympic gold medal-winning boxer, **Cassius Clay**, who later changed his name to Muhammad Ali, was so proud of his medal that he wore it all the time, *even in bed.*

Tiny Turkish Naim Suleymanoglu was weightlifting's first triple Olympic champion, winning three Games in a row. By the age of 16, he could lift **three times his own body weight**, even though he was only 150 cm tall, roughly the height of a ten-year-old boy.

The heaviest weight ever lifted by a woman is 186 kilograms – that's the same as **two full-grown men**.

Yasuhiro Yamashita, won his Olympic Judo title in 1984 with such a bad leg injury that his opponent had to help him up to the top step to receive his gold medal.

In the ancient Olympics, wrestlers **covered themselves in animal fat.** This made them very greasy so it was hard for their opponents to get a grip.

In 1912, the wrestling semi-final between Russia's Martin Klein and Finland's Alfred Asikainen lasted for **an incredible 11 hours!**

In 2004, Iranian weightlifter Hossein Rezazadeh lifted **263.5 kilograms** – the heaviest weight ever lifted by a human being in a weightlifting competition.

The heaviest oarsman ever in the Oxford–
Cambridge Boat Race was Thorsten
Engelmann in the 2007 Cambridge boat.
He weighed in at 110.8 kilograms.

OUCH!

It's **dangerous work** being a referee. In 1973, an angry player bit Italian referee Marcello Donadini so hard in the back that he had to be taken to hospital.

A referee at a friendly match in Brazil got out a gun and shot a player who argued with him, before escaping on horseback.

During the 2011 Tour de France, a French television car knocked straight into one of the cyclists, who then crashed into another cyclist and sent him straight into a **barbed wire fence**. Both riders were badly injured but they still got back in the saddle and carried on with the race.

Golfer Lee Trevino was once **struck by lightning** while playing, damaging his back.

If a squash ball hits you hard enough in the eye, it can burst your eyeball open.

Yeuch!

Golfer John Daly was playing in the Dutch Open in 2002 and got a piece of glass in his hand. Instead of getting stitches, he just poured glue on the cut and carried on playing.

When Australian rugby player Ben Czisolowski had a wound near his eye that wouldn't heal, his doctor discovered **an opponent's tooth** in Ben's forehead!

Yuck!

At the 2011 Criterium du Dauphine cycle race, some of the riders **swerved and crashed** when a **herd of cows** wandered onto the road and caused a pile-up.

Boxer Mike Tyson once **bit off a chunk** of his opponent's right ear and spat it into the ring. Luckily, someone found the **missing piece of ear**, wrapped it up and gave it back.

At the 1988 Olympics, diver Greg Louganis cracked his head on the diving board, and had to have stitches – but he came back and won a gold medal a few days later!

Italian footballer, Luigi Riva, once kicked the ball so hard that he **broke the arm** of an unlucky spectator.

ANIMAL
ANTICS

The **poor pigeon** that got in the way when South African batsman Jacques Rudolph threw a ball back to his bowler was *instantly killed* and fell straight to the ground.

When horseflies invaded a rugby pitch in Cornwall, one of the players was so badly bitten that his leg swelled up and he had to go to hospital.

Just days before the World Cup in 1966, the **trophy was stolen** – it was eventually found at the bottom of a hedge in South London by a dog called **Pickles**.

There are lots of **bee colonies** at the Visakhapatnam cricket stadium in India. When the bees come out in swarms, all the players and spectators have to lie flat on the ground until they've gone!

At the Sea Life Aquarium in Oberhausen, Germany, **Paul the octopus predicted the outcome** of all of Germany's matches in the 2010 World Cup. Paul had to select **mussels** from boxes draped in the colours of the two teams about to play. He even correctly chose **Spain** as the World Cup winner!

At a cricket match in Tasmania, play had to be stopped when **camels from a nearby circus** charged onto the pitch – not once, but four times!

During the World Cup quarter-final between **England and Brazil** in 1962, a stray dog ran onto the pitch. England striker, Jimmy Greaves, caught the dog and carried him off the pitch to huge cheers from the crowd.

At the Olympics' Opening Ceremonies, doves used to be released as a **symbol of peace** ... until 1988, when some of the birds perched on the edge of the Olympic cauldron – and got **roasted**!

JARGON BUSTING

The word 'wicket' means 'small gate', and because cricket stumps look like little gates, they became known as 'wickets'.

When a cricket batsman scores no runs, it's called a **'duck'** because zero – 0 – is the shape of a duck egg. And when a batsman is out on the first ball, it's a **golden duck**.

'Catching a crab' is a phrase used when rowers get an oar stuck in the water and slow their boat down.

The Flamingo, Crane and Fishtail are all positions in **synchronised swimming**.

In **Japanese**, 'Judo' means 'the gentle way', 'Kung fu' means 'work' or 'training', 'Karate' means 'empty hand' and 'Sumo' means 'both rushing together'.

'Throw in the towel' means giving up before the fight is over. It comes from boxing – when the boxer's helper throws a towel into the ring to tell the referee that the boxer doesn't want to carry on any more.

'Cow Corner' is the name of an area of the cricket field where so few shots are played that it's thought cows could graze there undisturbed.

Badminton was originally called **'Poona'** because it came from the Indian town of Poona. But nobody liked that name in England, so it was renamed 'Badminton' after it was played at the Duke of Beaufort's Gloucestershire home, Badminton House.

In Californian **surfing talk**, 'cooking' means a really good wave, 'noodled' means exhausted, 'wipe out' means to fall off the board, and 'landlord' is a great white shark.

'Slam Dunk' is when a basketball player jumps up to the basket and slams the ball downwards into the net with one or both hands.

The word 'gymnastics' comes from the Greek for 'naked' – early gymnasts used to perform **without wearing any clothes**!

BRILLIANT
BALLS

A football is made up of **32** leather panels, held together by **642** stitches.

Golf balls used to be **made of feathers**, boiled up to make them soft, then stuffed into a leather pouch. But they didn't fly very far, so new balls were designed over the years.

Table tennis balls were once made of cork or rubber, but the rubber ball bounced too wildly and the cork ball didn't bounce enough. So in 1900 a hollow plastic ball was invented.

54

In the mid-Nineteenth Century, rugby balls were made from inflated **pigs' bladders**, which become oval-shaped when blown up. The balls have stayed the same shape ever since, only now they're made of leather!

For the first ever Wimbledon tennis tournament in 1902, all the balls were hand stitched – which meant that every ball **bounced differently**.

Tennis balls are **covered in cloth** – if all the cloth used for the balls at Wimbledon was laid out, it would cover a pitch the size of the **Millennium Stadium**.

One year, Wimbledon donated **350** tennis balls to the Wildlife Trust, who cut them open and used them as **nest boxes for harvest mice**.

Being a ball boy or ball girl at Wimbledon is a tough job. They train for eight hours a week for four months before the start of the tournament.

At 2.7 grams, the table tennis ball is the **lightest ball** in sport.

The heaviest balls are used in ten-pin bowling – 7-9 kilograms – and in the men's shotput – just over seven kilograms, the same weight as over 2,500 table tennis balls.

WACKY
RACES AND
STRANGE
SPORTS

At the **Bed Race** in Knaresborough, Yorkshire, teams of six people have to push a bed with one person on it through the town on four wheels, and finally **float it across a river!**

That's the only race Lazy Linda would ever do.

The annual **Mud Olympics** are held on the muddy banks of the Elbe River in Germany, with lots of silly sports like **mud-eel racing** and **boot tossing**.

In **Chess Boxing** you play a round of chess followed by a round of boxing, with 11 rounds to either checkmate your opponent – or knock him out!

The World Championship **Cockroach Races** take place in Queensland, Australia, every year. The races were first set up when two Australians claimed that the place they lived had the biggest cockroaches. To settle the argument, they both went home, came back with a cockroach, and decided to race them.

In the annual **Cheese Rolling** competition in Gloucester, England, you have to run down a steep hill **chasing your hunk of cheese**. The cheese rolls at speeds of up to 30 miles per hour, so it's a surprisingly **dangerous** sport!

To win the **World Gurning Championships**, all you have to do is pull the most **horrible** face.

Wow! I'd be sure to win that one.

Extreme Ironing is a British sport. The first Extreme Ironing World Championships, in which competitors iron their clothes at the same time as bungee jumping or mountain climbing, was held in Germany in 2002. Teams competed to win prizes like **washing machines**.

The slimiest sport ever is the **World Bog Snorkelling Championships** held every year in Wales. Competitors put on wet suits and snorkels, and the winner is the first to finish two laps of a dirty, water-filled trench.

The **World Cow Chip Throwing Contest** takes place every year in Oklahoma, USA. People come from all over the world **to throw cow poo**, and the record is over 55 metres – that's the same as **four double-decker** buses standing end to end!

I'd have a cow poo throwing contest, but throwing it at Stuck-Up Steve.

Kite-Fighting is played in India, Afghanistan, Pakistan, Thailand and South America. The aim is to see whose kite flies highest and longest. Players put **sharp** objects in their kites to try and **cut down** the other player's kite strings.

OLYMPIC
ESSENTIALS

The Olympics are held in a **different country** every four years.

The Olympic motto is **'Citius, Altius, Fortius'**, which means **'Faster, Higher, Stronger'**.

The Olympic symbol of **five interlocking circles** represents the bringing together of athletes from five continents: Africa, the Americas, Asia, Europe and Oceania.

The **United States** has won more medals at the Summer Games than any other country.

More than **1,800 medals** are awarded at the Olympics.

Sshh! Today's Olympic gold medals **are really silver**, covered with a thin coating of gold.

What a cheat.

Tug of War was an Olympic event between 1900 and 1920, but it was dropped after the US and British teams disagreed about the **type of shoes** they could wear.

In 1928 **women were allowed to compete** in track and field events for the first time, but so many of them collapsed at the end of the 800 metre race that the event was **banned until 1960**.

No medals were awarded in the ancient Olympics – the winner received an **olive wreath** to wear on his head.

NUMBER
CRUNCHING

A badminton player can run more than **one mile** during a single match.

Only three teams have won the FA Cup without letting in a single goal: The Wanderers in 1873, Preston North End in 1889, and Bury in 1903. **And Ashton Athletic . . . well, I'm sure they will one day.**

On average, each player in a football match has the ball for only **three minutes**.

The distance the competing boats cover in the Oxford–Cambridge Boat Race is exactly four miles and 374 yards. The current time record is 16 minutes and 19 seconds, set by Cambridge in 1998.

The **most red cards** ever handed out during one football match is **20**.

Only seven teams have played in **every Premier League season** since it began – Liverpool, Manchester United, Chelsea, Everton, Spurs, Arsenal and Aston Villa.

Roger Federer has won **a record-breaking 16** major men's tennis titles – the Australian Open four times, the French Open once, Wimbledon six times, and the US Open five times.

Basketball player, Shaquille O'Neal, is best known for his **enormous feet** – shoe size **22** – compared to the average shoe size for men, which is size 9.

Every year at the Wimbledon Lawn Tennis Championships, about **27,000 kilograms of strawberries** are eaten, together with **7,000 litres of cream**.

The Scottish Cup tie between Falkirk and Inverness Thistle in 1979 had to be **postponed 29 times** because of bad weather.

Oops! One billion golf balls are lost every year.

Every year **40 horses** race in the **Grand National** at Aintree and jump **30 fences**.

In June 2005, South African scuba diver Nuno Gomes dived to a depth of **over 318 metres**, the height of the **Eiffel Tower** in Paris.

In 2011, the Tour de France route was **2,131 miles long**, divided into 21 stages ranging from 14 to 140 miles. It would take **34 hours** to drive this far in a car.

Over 52,000 tennis balls are used during the Wimbledon Championship – and every single ball is **hand tested** by the manufacturers for its bounce.

In angling, the **heaviest fish** ever caught was a common carp. At 42.64 kilograms it was roughly the same weight as a ten-year-old girl.

Uruguay, with a population of just three million, is the **smallest nation** to have won the World Cup.

BRAINBUSTERS

At the annual World Chess Championships, games can last for hours or they can be over in just a few minutes.

The **longest chess game** on record was held in Yugoslavia in 1989 between Ivan Nikolic and Goran Arsovic – they played for **over 20 hours** and made **269 moves**, and no one won!

Believe it or not, there are **World Monopoly Championships**, which are held every four years.

At the 2009 World Monopoly Championships, 19-year-old Norwegian, Bjorn Halvard Knappskog, **playing with the iron**, won £12,200 (in real money!) in a game lasting **just over 40 minutes**.

Since 1991, the **World Scrabble Championships** have taken place every other year, with all the players using English. Separate French and Spanish World Championships also take place.

In 1998, the world's **largest game of Scrabble** took place in Britain's Wembley Stadium to celebrate the game's 50th anniversary. Each of the tiles measured **two-metres square** – about the size of a **king-size bed** – and it took two men to lift them.

One **angry scrabble player** took the Association of British Scrabble Players to court in 1995 for allowing too little time for him to **go to the toilet** between games at the Championships.

The first World Scrabble Championships in 1991 were held in London. But they got off to a very bad start when there were **no tiles to play with!**

SUPER
SPEEDY

The highest cycling speed recorded over the course of the Tour de France is just over **15 miles an hour**, by Lance Armstrong in 2005.

A top human sprinter can reach nearly **30 miles an hour** in a **ten-second sprint** race, but can't keep up this speed over more than 65 metres.

A galloping thoroughbred racehorse – can reach a maximum speed of 30 miles an hour for distances of **over a mile**.

Greyhounds race at top speeds of 45 miles per hour. They are the second fastest animals in the world, after cheetahs.

In 2007 in Brazil, Douglas da Silva achieved the **fastest skateboard speed** from a standing position – just over 70 miles an hour.

Olympic downhill skiers can get up to speeds of 80 miles an hour.

The world's top table tennis players can smash the ball at speeds of more than 100 miles an hour.

In the **Le Mans 24-Hour Race**, one of the world's **most extreme motorsport events**, cars race for 24 hours and travel more than 3,000 miles at speeds of over 125 miles an hour.

Race cars can be driven at speeds of nearly 230 miles an hour.

A **badminton shuttlecock** easily travels at up to 112 miles an hour.

SCARY
SPORTS

Downhill skiing is fast and furious, with skiers reaching speeds of around 90 miles an hour down the mountains.

Aaaah!

The athletes from Sparta were scary! Spartan babies were left out in the cold to make them tough, and the boys and girls had to **practise fighting** every day.

In **jousting**, horsemen gallop towards each other with a pole and try to knock one another off their horse. This was a popular sport in medieval times.

New Zealand rugby teams perform a **war dance** called a 'haka', based on a Maori war chant, to **scare their opponents**.

Skydiving isn't as dangerous as you'd have thought. In 2004, stings by **bees, wasps and hornets** killed 52 Americans, while skydiving killed 21.

Ping-pong doesn't sound a very frightening sport, but it was **banned in Russia** from 1930 to 1950 because it was believed to be harmful to the eyes.

Hundreds of years ago on a South Pacific island, tribesmen tested their courage by **tying vines to their feet** and launching themselves from a great height – an early form of **bungee jumping**.

In Spain, bulls are bred to be especially **bad-tempered** for the sport of bullfighting.

FASTEST, LONGEST, TALLEST, HIGHEST...

The **longest ever tennis match** took place at Wimbledon in 2010 when John Isner of the United States beat Nicolas Mahut of France in a match that lasted **11 hours and 5 minutes, played over 3 days**.

Ivo Karlovic, from Croatia, has the world's **fastest tennis serve**, a staggering 156 miles an hour. A hurricane travelling at this speed could blow the roof off a building!

In 1950/51 Leslie Compton became the **oldest footballer** to make his debut for England when he played against Wales aged 38 years and two months. Today, footballers reach their peak in their mid–twenties.

The **heaviest elite sportsperson** in the world was sumo wrestler Konishiki Yasokichi, nicknamed **the Dump Truck** – in 1996 he tipped the scales at nearly 285 kilograms. That's more than a quarter of a tonne.

The **shortest person** to play tennis at Wimbledon was British player, Miss C.G. Hoahing, who was just 145 cm tall. Today, most of the female players are at least 30 cm taller than Miss Hoahing.

The **tallest basketball player** ever was Libyan Suleiman Ali Nashnush at a massive 257 cm, which is **even bigger than your front door!**

The **world's fastest man** is currently Jamaican, Usain Bolt, nicknamed **Lightning Bolt**. Bolt's top running speed is an astonishing 28 miles per hour.

The **longest jumper** is Mike Powell of USA who in 1991 jumped 8.95 metres, about the length of **five baths** laid end to end, beating Bob Beamon's 22-year-old world record of 8.9 metres.

The **quickest bowler** in cricket is Shoaib Akhtar of Pakistan who has bowled at nearly 100 miles an hour – that's **faster than a cheetah** can run or you can drive on the motorway.

In 1985, Germany's Boris Becker was the **youngest winner** of the men's singles at Wimbledon at the age of 17.

Cuban high jumper Javier Sotomayor cleared an incredible 2.45 metres in 1993, higher than the ceiling in most houses – and the **highest jump ever achieved** by a human being.

Brazil has won the World Cup **five times**, more than any other country.

German canoeist Birgit Fischer was both the **youngest ever Olympic canoeing champion** at 18 years old, and the oldest ever at 42.

Badminton is the **fastest racquet sport** in the world, with a shuttlecock leaving the racquet at almost 200 miles per hour!!

In 1957, Stanley Matthews became the **oldest footballer** to play for England at the age of 42. He continued playing Division One football until he was 50 years old.

In 1997, aged 16, Martina Hingis became the **youngest women's tennis player** to be the **World Number One**.

Cesar Cielo holds the world record of 20.91 seconds for the **men's 50 metres freestyle** – a race so fast, that many swimmers **hold their breath** from start to finish.

STRANGE
BUT TRUE

A craze among Chelsea fans for **waving sticks of celery during football matches** began when the fans used to pinch celery from allotments before away matches. But the craze got out of hand and in 2007 anyone caught trying to sneak in celery was threatened with **a life ban**.

In 1953, driver Tim Flock entertained the crowd at the Hickory Motor Speedway in America by **racing with his pet monkey** sitting in the seat beside him.

During a **football match** between Arsenal and Moscow at White Hart Lane in 1945, it was so foggy that the Russian goalie ran into the goal post and was **knocked unconscious.** When a spectator took over in goal, **no one even noticed!**

In the 1938 World Cup semi-final, Italian player, **Guiseppe Meazza's shorts fell down** when he was taking a penalty shot! He calmly pulled his shorts back up and scored.

Footballer Fernando d'Ercoli once got so angry when he was **given a red card**, he snatched the card from the referee and **ate it.**

In 1971, **golf** became the only sport to be played **on the moon** when Alan Shepard hit a golf ball, using a golf club head he had smuggled inside his space suit.

In 1995, a **Manchester City fan** used to celebrate City goals by **swinging dead chickens** around his head, until he was banned from bringing the birds.

At the ancient Olympics, men competed **in the nude**.

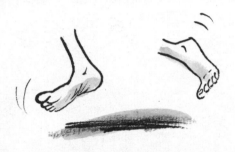

Can you believe it? In ancient Japan, contests were held to see who could **fart the loudest** and longest.

Rude Ralph told me that.

A man in Hawaii has invented a three-player table for table tennis, calling it 'Tri-Pong'. It has see-through plastic 'nets' to divide the table into three wedges, one for each player.

In 2005, American skier Lindsey Vonn won a World Cup in France. She was offered the choice of an additional **$1,200 in prize money or a cow**. She chose the cow!

Bye!

WORLD CUP QUIZ

I. How many players are there in a football team?

2. How many countries played in the 2014 World Cup qualifying rounds?

3. How many countries play in the World Cup Finals?

4. How many players can a team have as potential substitutes?

5. Which country has won the World Cup the most times?

6. Which player has scored the most World Cup Finals goals?

7. Which country has scored the most World Cup goals over all?

8. What's the most number of goals ever scored in a match in the World Cup Finals?

9. How often is the World Cup staged?

10. When did England last win the World Cup?

11. Which 2 countries have reached the final the most times?

12. Which country has been runner-up the most times?

13. Which 2 countries have won consecutive titles?

14. What colours will feature on the official 2014 World Cup football?

15. Which country is hosting the 2014 World Cup?

16. How many different stadiums will host World Cup Finals matches in 2014?

17. Where will the World Cup be held in 2018?

18. How many times has the UK hosted the World Cup?

19. Which country won the last World Cup, held in 2010?

20. The official name of the World Cup is the FIFA World Cup. What do the initials FIFA stand for?

21. Which is the only country to have played in every World Cup tournament?

22. How many World Cup tournaments have there been?

23. Who is the current England manager?

24. What country is the current England football manager from?

25. 4 teams from the UK aim to qualify for the World Cup – who are they?

Answers over the page . . .

Answers

1. 11 players – from a squad of 23

2. 208 teams

3. 32 teams

4. 7

5. Brazil (5 times)

6. Ronaldo of Brazil, scorer of 15 World Cup Finals goals

7. Brazil, with 210 goals in World Cup tournaments to date

8. 12 (Austria beat Switzerland 7–5 in 1954)

9. Every 4 years

10. 1966

11. Both Germany and Brazil have reached the final 7 times

12. Germany

13. Brazil and Italy

14. White, green and yellow

15. Brazil

16. 12

17. Russia

18. Once

19. Spain

20. *Fédération Internationale de Football Association*

21. Brazil

22. 19

23. Roy Hodgson

24. England

25. England, Northern Ireland, Scotland and Wales

HORRID HENRY BOOKS

Horrid Henry
Horrid Henry and the Secret Club
Horrid Henry Tricks the Tooth Fairy
Horrid Henry's Nits
Horrid Henry Gets Rich Quick
Horrid Henry's Haunted House
Horrid Henry and the Mummy's Curse
Horrid Henry's Revenge
Horrid Henry and the Bogey Babysitter
Horrid Henry's Stinkbomb
Horrid Henry's Underpants
Horrid Henry Meets the Queen
Horrid Henry and the Mega-Mean Time Machine
Horrid Henry and the Football Fiend
Horrid Henry's Christmas Cracker
Horrid Henry and the Abominable Snowman
Horrid Henry Robs the Bank
Horrid Henry Wakes the Dead
Horrid Henry Rocks
Horrid Henry and the Zombie Vampire
Horrid Henry's Nightmare

Early Readers

Don't Be Horrid, Henry!
Horrid Henry's Birthday Party
Horrid Henry's Holiday
Horrid Henry's Underpants
Horrid Henry Gets Rich Quick
Horrid Henry and the Football Fiend
Horrid Henry's Nits
Horrid Henry and Moody Margaret
Horrid Henry's Thank You Letter
Horrid Henry Reads a Book
Horrid Henry's Car Journey
Moody Margaret's School

Activity Books

Visit Horrid Henry's website at **www.horridhenry.co.uk** for competitions, games, downloads and a monthly newsletter.